SELF TALK WORKBOOK

Daily Reflections & Writing Prompt Journal for Positive Thinking

by ASTON SANDERSON

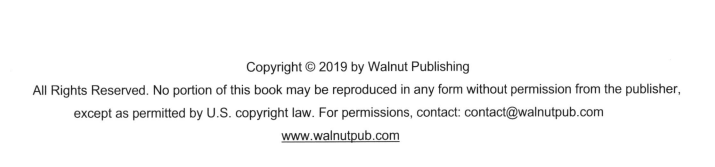

Table of Contents

1 - Introduction ... 1

2- What is Self Talk? ... 3

3 - Why is Negative Self Talk Bad? ... 11

4 - Benefits of Changing Self Talk ... 12

5 - How We Will Change Your Self Talk ... 15

6 - The First Step is Awareness ... 17

7 - You Are Not Your Thoughts ... 20

8 - Questioning a Negative Thought ... 22

9 - The Opposite Thought ... 33

10 - Perspective ... 36

11 - Naming ... 39

12 - Self-Compassion ... 41

13 - Constructive Negative Self Talk ... 43

14 - Outside Influences to Consider ... 44

15 - Conclusion ... 48

About the Author ... 51

CHAPTER 1 - Introduction

Welcome to the Self Talk Workbook!

First things first — I recommend you also buy "Self Talk," the guide that serves as a companion to this book, to get a deeper reading on the concepts we will introduce in these pages. The books work best together when you can read a chapter in "Self Talk" and then look at the exercises in this Workbook.

However, do not fret if you only have this Workbook! You can still get started learning about how to change your patterns of thinking. We'll discuss aspects of self talk in this book; they will just not be explored as in-depth as in the "Self Talk" book.

This journal focuses less on reading and more on writing! It is interactive, and meant to get you thinking and exploring your own mental chatter through a fresh lens.

We'll explore how your self-talk currently works through writing prompts and reflections, and then we'll look at how you can change those thinking patterns to better serve your life.

We all want to achieve our goals, find love, do meaningful work, be healthy and be kind to others. But often, we're own own worst enemies when it comes to actually making these things happen.

With this book, I want to help you better achieve the things you want in your life by first being kinder to yourself in your thoughts. Every thing you do must first start as a thought in your head, right?

Your timeline for your journey through this workbook is self-guided; you can choose to spend a week on each chapter, really deeply connecting with the ideas and writing more about the prompts outside of these pages, if you need additional paper.

Or, you can see this book as a quick, two-week bootcamp to get your thoughts back on track and make yourself a more positive and resilient person.

However the book works best for you is how you should approach it.

Additionally, if there are some exercises you find unhelpful, feel free to tailor the exercises that you like best. Do not feel bad if not everything connects with you personally; this book was designed with everyone in mind. And since we are all different, some of us will gravitate to certain exercises more than others. Just because you didn't fully complete each exercise in a chapter does not mean you have failed! In fact, it means you can spend more time on the exercises you do feel make a difference for you. And that's what I suggest you do.

One last note: Sometimes the exercises will be difficult, but I ask you to please not give up or be afraid of confronting the mean voice in your head.

It can be scary: *"Who do you think you are?"* the voice may ask. Your negative self talk may say, *"You can't get rid of this way of thinking, and you're silly for even trying."*

But having negative thoughts is something each of us struggles with. Learning how to be aware of them, how to harness them, and how to have a healthier inner mental life is what this book is all about.

I hope you enjoy, and please let me know what you thought of this book. I truly love to hear from readers (and I read every review left on my Amazon page) so please feel free to reach out to me at aston@walnutpub.com. (And also please leave a review :))

Sincerely,
Aston Sanderson

Disclaimer: If you struggle with mental issues outside the scope of this book — clinical depression, overwhelming anxiety, or anything else that disrupts your daily living of life — I urge you to seek professional medical help from a licensed therapist, doctor, or reach out to a trusted friend or family member who can help you find help. I am not a doctor, and the exercises in this book do not stand-in for help from a qualified mental health professional.

CHAPTER 2 - What is Self Talk?

For this book, we'll define self talk as:

> **Self talk is your internal monologue.**
> **It is the thoughts that go through your head on a daily basis.**
> **Usually, it is how you talk to yourself *about* yourself.**

Whether or not we are conscious of it, we all have self talk. For the exercises in this chapter, we'll look at 7 types of self talk, and leave space for you to write down examples of each kind.

If you are ready to dive into writing down your own negative self talk, go right ahead. Take note that writing down the negative things you've said to yourself can be painful, so proceed with caution. We'll get to writing down your specific self talk in a later chapter.

For now, if you find it too uncomfortable or too much work to write down your own self talk, just make up examples. You can draw from TV shows or movies, books, or think of things you've overheard. You can also just entirely make them up.

This chapter is all about learning what self talk is. Let's dive in to the 7 types of negative self talk.

7 Types of Self Talk

Filtering	Catastrophizing	Personalizing	Polarizing	Rehashing	Rehearsing	Blaming
#1	#2	#3	#4	#5	#6	#7

#1: Filtering

Filtering means that when 10 good things happen to us, and one bad thing, we only remember the one bad thing.

Example: "Today was a terrible day because I burned the lasagna for dinner and it was ruined!"
(Forget about that nice surprise phone call from my sister, the beautiful weather, or all the other chores around the house that went perfectly fine.)

Write out some examples of your own:

#2: Catastrophizing

> When one thing goes wrong, it seems everything goes wrong, or you blow that one thing way out of proportion.

Example: "If the weather won't be nice on our vacation, then what's the point of even going? This always happens to us. Why can't we do nice things as a family? They always get ruined. We can't afford it anyway. Now it's a waste of money and time."

Write out some examples of your own:

_____

_____

_____

_____

_____

_____

_____

_____

_____

#3: Personalizing

Making external events a reflection of you, even if they aren't. When bad things happen, you will find a reason that you are to blame or caused it. Also known as internalizing.

Example: It was my fault my team's work presentation didn't go over well today. My contribution was the weakest; if I wasn't on the team, it would have been very different. Even though there are 12 people on the team, I know I am solely to blame.

Write out some examples of your own:

_____

_____

_____

_____

_____

_____

_____

_____

_____

_____

_____

#4: Polarizing

Events or traits are seen as either 100% good or 100% bad.
There is no in-between or gray area.

Example: "My sense of humor always gets me in trouble! I can't believe what I said today to Jim. Forget all the people I usually make laugh; it's just not worth it for slipping up sometimes."

Write out some examples of your own:

_____

_____

_____

_____

_____

_____

_____

_____

#5: Rehashing

Also known as ruminating or dwelling. Thinking about the past, but in a negative, unproductive and circular manner.

Example: "The cause of all my problems was the decision to skip the beach outing that day. If I had gone, I wouldn't have grown apart from Rick and the guys, and I wouldn't have had that fight with Lisa. If only I could go back to that day and make a different choice..."

Write out some examples of your own:

_____

_____

_____

_____

_____

_____

_____

_____

_____

_____

_____

#6: Rehearsing

The opposite side of the coin of rehashing. Rehearsing is thinking about the future, but in a circular and unproductive fashion as well.

Example: "When I go to the party, I'll have to talk to new people, and if I tell them I'm a high school teacher, they'll ask me what I teach, and I hate talking about math outside of work, so I'll just lie ... No, I'll say the truth but redirect the conversation ... No, I'll ..."

Write out some examples of your own:

#7: Blaming

 Blaming happens when we feel responsible for someone else's feelings of pain, or our own normal human feelings.

Example: "Why do I have down days sometimes? I'm just too weak. I shouldn't ever feel sad, it's because I'm defective."

Write out some examples of your own:

_____

_____

_____

_____

_____

_____

_____

_____

_____

_____

CHAPTER 3 - Why is Negative Self Talk Bad?

Now that you have recognized some types of negative self talk, what's the big deal? It's just a few pessimistic thoughts, right?

But negative self talk becomes such an ingrained pattern in our head that we have trouble snapping out of it, and seeing things in a new light.

Negative thinking patterns prevent us from feeling good about ourselves, achieving our goals, being happy, and having healthy relationships.

In What Areas of Your Life Do You Have Negative Self Talk?

In this exercise, circle areas of your life where you know you experience negative self talk. If one is not listed, write in your own on the line. Don't worry about how many you circle — just be honest with yourself.

Romantic Relationship/Dating   Family Relationships   Friendship   Appearance/Weight

Work Performance/Job   Productivity   Hobbies   How You Spend Free Time   Habits

Intelligence   Social Skills   Self Image   Athleticism   Popularity   Personality

Sexuality   Interests   The Past   The Future   Confidence   My Current Self Talk!

CHAPTER 4 - Benefits of Changing Self Talk

In the last chapter, we discussed how negative self talk harms us, but here's the good news: How can positive self talk help us?

In this chapter's exercises, we'll explore in what ways you'd like better self talk to improve your life.

In the boxes available, use the space to draw a picture, journal stream-of-consciousness style, brainstorm words or feelings, or write full sentences. However you respond to the prompt is correct! Just get the thoughts out.

You Can Become More **Resilient**

 Think of an area you struggle with in your life. Maybe certain relationships, or work performance, your health, etc. What if you could not fail in this area? What would you attempt to achieve? How would life be better if this area was easy?

More time for **Creativity & Enjoyment**

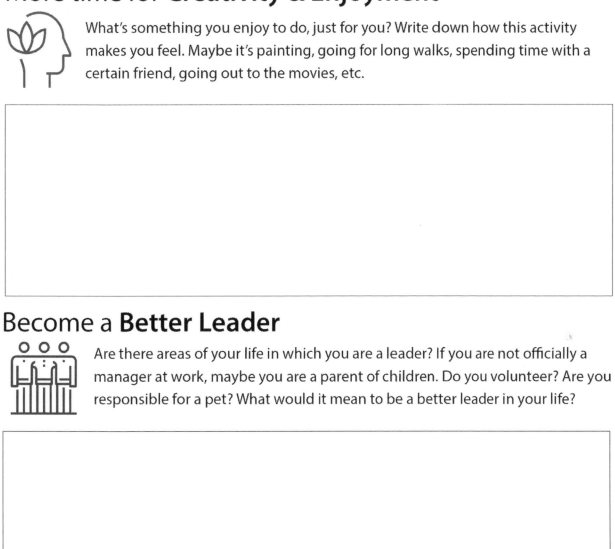

What's something you enjoy to do, just for you? Write down how this activity makes you feel. Maybe it's painting, going for long walks, spending time with a certain friend, going out to the movies, etc.

Become a **Better Leader**

Are there areas of your life in which you are a leader? If you are not officially a manager at work, maybe you are a parent of children. Do you volunteer? Are you responsible for a pet? What would it mean to be a better leader in your life?

Achieve Your **Goals**

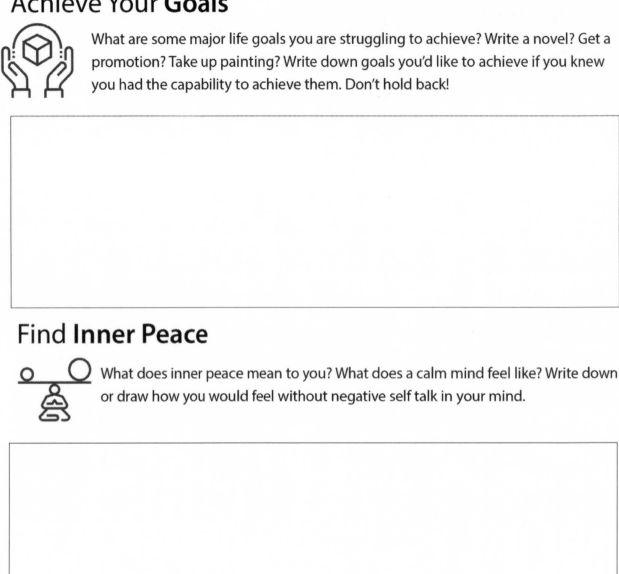

What are some major life goals you are struggling to achieve? Write a novel? Get a promotion? Take up painting? Write down goals you'd like to achieve if you knew you had the capability to achieve them. Don't hold back!

Find **Inner Peace**

What does inner peace mean to you? What does a calm mind feel like? Write down or draw how you would feel without negative self talk in your mind.

CHAPTER 5 - How We Will Change Your Self Talk

In this chapter, we will outline the right mindset you need as you begin the task of changing your self talk.

Fixed Mindset vs. Growth Mindset

A fixed mindset means that you believe that who you are today is basically who you have always been and who you will always be. When someone has a growth mindset, they acknowledge that they are constantly changing.

For this exercise, write down some examples of a fixed vs. growth mindset in your own life.

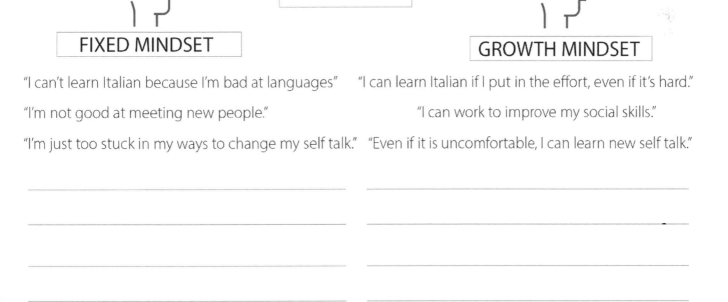

EXAMPLES

FIXED MINDSET

"I can't learn Italian because I'm bad at languages"

"I'm not good at meeting new people."

"I'm just too stuck in my ways to change my self talk."

GROWTH MINDSET

"I can learn Italian if I put in the effort, even if it's hard."

"I can work to improve my social skills."

"Even if it is uncomfortable, I can learn new self talk."

Habit Building

To change your self talk, the best way is to start with extremely small, achievable "mini-habits."

The circuits in your brain are like paths through a forest. Your current habits are the paths that have already been cleared, so it's easy to walk down them again and again. Making new habits is like hacking through the brush, cutting down thick weeds and trees to clear a new path.

At first, making new habits and thought patterns will be challenging. But eventually, they will be as easy to walk down as the thought patterns you have now.

Like lifting weights, you can't change everything overnight. You have to start with the lightest weights and slowly build up strength over time. Don't be discouraged if you don't feel progress right away with changing your negative thinking; this is a marathon that will last for life, not a quick sprint for a week or two.

The new, healthy thinking patterns you create can last a lifetime, if you take care of them.

Activity: Reminders to Help You Build a Habit of Noticing Self Talk

For this chapter, you've got a bit of homework outside of this workbook. Set up reminders to notice your self talk every day. This will help you in the next chapter, when we start recording your actual self talk. Some ideas for reminders are:

- *Set a reminder on your phone*
- *Put a Post-It note on your mirror, or where you'll see it every day*
- *Keep this workbook next on your nightstand so you open it every night before bed*
- *Your ideas!*

Now, take action! Set one (or more) of these reminders. It shouldn't take more than 5 minutes, so get it done! Write it down, go do it, and then come back and check it completed.

Reminder(s) I Chose: **Set Reminder?**

_____   ☐

_____   ☐

CHAPTER 6 - The First Step is Awareness

The first step to remaking your self talk is to be aware of it. This sounds simple, but can actually be quite difficult when we're lost in a storm of self-criticism, self-doubt, and other negative tendencies that we're so used to, we can't even see them.

Use the reminders you set up in the last chapter to start noticing and writing down your self talk in this one.

Record Your Self Talk

 Record some of the thoughts that you notice throughout the next few days or week. Noticing positive self talk is good, too! Just notice what thoughts you have. We've started you off with some examples.

DATE	SELF TALK	POSITIVE OR NEGATIVE?	
3/12	I can't believe I forgot the eggs! This always happens to me.	+	(−)
3/12	I am proud of myself for staying calm while calling the frustrating cable company	(+)	−
3/13	Ugh, I hate my arm flab	+	(−)
		+	−
		+	−
		+	−
		+	−
		+	−

DATE   SELF TALK

POSITIVE OR
NEGATIVE?

+   -

+   -

+   -

+   -

+   -

+   -

+   -

+   -

+   -

+   -

+   -

+   -

+   -

+   -

+   -

+   -

+   -

+   -

DATE   SELF TALK

	POSITIVE OR NEGATIVE?	
	+	-
	+	-
	+	-
	+	-
	+	-
	+	-
	+	-
	+	-
	+	-
	+	-
	+	-
	+	-
	+	-
	+	-
	+	-
	+	-
	+	-
	+	-

CHAPTER 7 - You Are Not Your Thoughts

You are not your thoughts — in fact, maybe your thoughts are not even *your* thoughts! All that negative self talk came from somewhere, and even though I'm sure you're a very smart and creative person, I'm pretty sure you can't take credit for *all* your negative self talk.

I'm betting some of your self talk came from other places: Society at large, popular culture, a TV show, someone in your family, a bully from childhood, your mom, an overly critical friend (and therefore not a good friend, but that's a subject for another book...)

Thoughts That Are Not Your Own:

 Record some of the thoughts you have that you think you originally heard from another source, and identify the source. You can use some of your self talk you recorded in the last chapter.

THOUGHT	ORIGINAL SOURCE
I'll never make enough money in the field I love; I need to get a 'real' job	*My dad*

THOUGHT

ORIGINAL SOURCE

CHAPTER 8 - Questioning a Negative Thought

This chapter will be a bit more intense — it's about throwing your thought in the interrogation room and getting to the bottom of things! You can deconstruct a thought by asking it a long list of questions. Like always, use those you find helpful; skip one if you are unsure about it. But try to try them all at least once! On these first two pages, I'll show you an example. Then it's your turn.

Thought Interrogation

Negative Self Talk: *I am a failure because I am single.*

• **Who is this important to?** Being single is important to me. I'd like to share my life with someone. But it seems more important to my parents, who want me to be married like my brother and sister. Maybe it is more important to them, actually.

• **How much does this matter in the long run?** I want to eventually get married, so it matters in the long run. But I guess in "the long run" I have more time to find a partner.

• **Is my response an overreaction?** I do have other areas of my life I feel successful in, like my career.

• **Am I overgeneralizing? Does my thought apply to everyone who is similar in this way to me?** Is everyone who is single a failure? No, there are a lot of people who choose to be single or are happy being single.

• **What is the concrete evidence for this thought?** I feel bad when I go to family gatherings without a partner. But those are my feelings. My parents always ask when I'm getting married. So their question is evidence that they think I'm a failure. No, it is concrete evidence that they want me to have a partner.

• Am I viewing things in terms of absolutes? (Remember the "polarizing" type of negative self talk from the first chapter) Yes. I am defining myself as a failure because I am single.

• Should it be more of a gray area? Yes. I am not an absolute failure in every area of life, I guess.

• Am I assuming the thoughts or feelings of others? I am assuming that my parents think I'm a failure because they allude to wanting me to have a partner.

• Am I using cruel language? Failure is pretty harsh.

• If I were having a positive thought about this, how would I interpret things? I have a lot of time to pursue my own interests being single, and maybe I am doing so well at work because I don't have to worry about making extra time for a partner right now.

• What is the worst thing that could result from this? How likely is that to actually happen? If it did happen, what would be the next step I would take? The worst thing that could happen is that I stay single forever. It could happen but it seems everyone finds someone at some point, so there is a chance I will find a partner. If I did end up single forever, the next step I would take is maybe adopting a child on my own.

• Could the situation or feeling be worse? Yes. I could be "older" with "less time" to find a partner. My grandma even found a new boyfriend at the nursing home a few years after my grandpa died. I have had dating experience before, it would be harder to date without my previous experience. I could live in a small town, instead of this big city, where there are more opportunities for dating.

• Is this thinking going to help me achieve my goals? Thinking I'm a failure probably won't attract a partner.

• What would help me feel better or think a different way? I could try to not feel so ashamed about being single. Maybe then I'd put myself out there more for dating.

• **What can I learn from this thought?** I can learn that being single is a sore spot for me and something I'm sensitive about. Probably because my parents put pressure on me.

• **What is another way to interpret the situation? What would that mean?** Maybe I am less of a "failure" than my friends who got married too young and are already divorced. Though it's not nice to think of my friends as failures. That means if it's not nice to call them failures, it's not nice to call myself a failure.

• **What physical evidence for this exists, and how much is my feeling or perception?** I can't think of any physical evidence. I don't have a ring on my finger? That seems like a silly reason to be a failure, not wearing a piece of jewelry on a certain finger.

• **What is the evidence for my conclusion?** I guess there is no evidence, I just don't like going to events with friends where I know everyone will be a couple except me.

• **How would a friend talk to me about this thought?** A friend would probably tell me I need to date more and am not putting myself out there enough if I am not happy being single.

• **How would someone from a different culture or upbringing feel about this thought?** I guess some people have arranged marriages in other cultures and would probably want to be single like me.

• **If I am ruminating on a choice I made in the past, am I prepared to take steps to make a change right now? Otherwise I need to let it go. But if I am willing to make change, then I need to take those steps.** I sometimes wish I hadn't broken up with my boyfriend and imagine what our life would be like still together. But I don't want to get back with him, as our relationship was not good. So, no, I am not willing to make a change, so I should stop wasting time daydreaming about not having broken up with him. I should focus on the future instead.

Thought Interrogation

Negative Self Talk: _____

• Who is this important to?

• How much does this matter in the long run?

• Is my response an overreaction?

• Am I overgeneralizing?

• What is the concrete evidence for this thought?

• Am I viewing things in terms of absolutes? (Remember the "polarizing" type of negative self talk from the second chapter.) Should it be more of a gray area?

• Am I assuming the thoughts or feelings of others?

• Am I using cruel language?

• If I were having a positive thought about this, how would I interpret things?

• What is the worst thing that could result from this? How likely is that to actually happen? If it did happen, what would be the next step I would take?

• Could the situation or feeling be worse?

• Is this thinking going to help me achieve my goals?

• What would help me feel better or think a different way?

• What can I learn from this thought?

• What is another way to interpret the situation? What would that mean?

• What physical evidence for this exists, and how much is my feeling or perception?

• What is the evidence for my conclusion?

• How would a friend talk to me about this thought?

• How would someone from a different culture or upbringing feel about this thought?

• If I am ruminating on a choice I made in the past, am I prepared to take steps to make a change right now? Otherwise I need to let it go. But if I am willing to make change, then I need to take those steps.

BIGGEST TAKEAWAYS FROM THIS INTERROGATION?

Thought Interrogation

Negative Self Talk: _____

• Who is this important to?

• How much does this matter in the long run?

• Is my response an overreaction?

• Am I overgeneralizing?

• What is the concrete evidence for this thought?

• Am I viewing things in terms of absolutes? (Remember the "polarizing" type of negative self talk from the second chapter.) Should it be more of a gray area?

- Am I assuming the thoughts or feelings of others?

- Am I using cruel language?

- If I were having a positive thought about this, how would I interpret things?

- What is the worst thing that could result from this? How likely is that to actually happen? If it did happen, what would be the next step I would take?

- Could the situation or feeling be worse?

- Is this thinking going to help me achieve my goals?

- What would help me feel better or think a different way?

- What can I learn from this thought?

- What is another way to interpret the situation? What would that mean?

- What physical evidence for this exists, and how much is my feeling or perception?

- What is the evidence for my conclusion?

- How would a friend talk to me about this thought?

• How would someone from a different culture or upbringing feel about this thought?

• If I am ruminating on a choice I made in the past, am I prepared to take steps to make a change right now? Otherwise I need to let it go. But if I am willing to make change, then I need to take those steps.

BIGGEST TAKEAWAYS FROM THIS INTERROGATION?

CHAPTER 9 - Opposite Thoughts

In this chapter, we'll look not only at a favorite game from childhood — playing the "Opposite Game" — but also take some time to appreciate your strengths. Let's go!

Creating Opposite Thoughts

 When we have negative self talk, one of the easiest strategies to use to try to flip our thoughts around is to think: What is the opposite of what I've just thought about myself or this situation? Notice from the examples below that it can be small — a sandwich — or big — just being grateful for being alive. When constructing your opposite statements, it is helpful to avoid absolute statements. Avoid words like "always" or "never." Life is often somewhere in-between.

YOUR SELF TALK	OPPOSITE THOUGHTS
Today is a crappy day because I forgot to send an important email this morning	• Today is a great day because I have a job • Today is a great day because I have learned a valuable lesson about setting reminders for my most important tasks • Today is a great day because I had a nice lunch (a delicious sandwich) with a new coworker • Today is a great day because I am alive
I don't like my body	• My eyes allow me to see a beautiful sunset • My feet allow me to walk down the street • Me brain allows me to read or watch TV • My nerves and skin allow me to feel the touch of another person, whether it is romantic or just a hug • My ears allow me to hear a song I like

YOUR SELF TALK

OPPOSITE THOUGHTS

Remembering Your Strengths

 When you say something negative about one of your attributes, like that you are bad at meeting new people, the opposite thought may be to call upon your strengths. But if you truly *aren't* good at meeting new people, don't write the opposite — that you are great at meeting new people — as it wouldn't be true. Instead, remember fixed vs. growth mindset phrases from Chapter 5. See the example below:

YOUR SELF TALK

OPPOSITE THOUGHTS

I am not good at
meeting new people

- I am great at meeting new people
- I am working on improving my social skills
- I am proud of myself for getting out of my comfort zone to meet new people, when it is an activity I recognize makes me nervous
- I am grateful I only feel that my skills could improve for meeting new people, and that I don't have a fear of leaving my house or diagnosed social anxiety, which I imagine would be worse

For a feel-goof exercise to close out this chapter, write down some of your strengths!

(If you're having trouble, think about what people who love you would say about you — great smile, infectious laugh, always on time, generous, artistic, etc.)

CHAPTER 10 - Perspective

We've already practiced taking a step back from thoughts and dis-identifying with them. Now we will practice taking a step back even from ourselves, to focus on others and get some perspective about our place in the world.

Think About Others

 When you are throwing a pity party, a good thing to do is take a step back from yourself. If you always compare yourself to someone who is better off than you, you should also compare yourself to people who are worse off. How bad do you really have it? Do you have a roof over your head, food in your belly? Then you have it better than so much of the world. Of course, your problems are still valid, but this can be a calming tactic.

For this exercise, free-write, draw, brainstorm, or just put down whatever you feel about gaining some perspective on what gets you down — by thinking about others.

Remember That People Are Self-Focused

 The second tactic to help you gain some perspective from your negative self talk is to ask yourself: Who cares? Remember that everyone is more focused on themselves than they are on anyone else. Aren't you reading a book about the way you talk to yourself inside your head? That we all have these constant thoughts about ourselves should tell you a lot about how self-focused people are. Remembering that people are often worrying about themselves can take some of the pressure off of you.

Once again, just express some feelings, thoughts or drawings about how much you worry about what other people think, and how freeing yourself from that can help you gain perspective:

Laugh at Yourself

Life can be pretty absurd. Humor is a good antidote to feeling bad.

For example, if you're feeling a bit self-conscious at the gym, and it makes it hard for you to get up off the couch, you can try to think about how absurd the idea of a gym is. Humans evolved fighting for survival in the African plains. Today, humans are pretty comfortable, comparably. So comfortable, in fact, that we build big boxes with machines of varying movements just to exercise our rested bodies. What would cave people think of the muscled and toned people who spend so much time at the gym to make their body look a certain way? It's a bit absurd if you take a step back from it. That can give you just a little boost of confidence and a "who cares" attitude to get to the gym and not feel so intimidated.

Once again, be free in this box to throw some humor into the things that cause you stress:

CHAPTER 11 - Naming

In this chapter, we'll look at two new methods to gain distance from self talk.

Talk to Yourself in the Third Person

 Talking to yourself in the third person lets you be more objective. We are often better at seeing our friends' problems more clearly than our own, and better at giving advice to friends than to ourselves. If you say "you" instead of "I" when you talk to yourself in your head, you can be a bit more objective.

SELF TALK IN 1st-PERSON

I am feeling nervous about my date tonight

I don't like my new haircut

SELF TALK IN 3rd-PERSON

You are feeling nervous about your date tonight

You don't like your new haircut

Name Your Inner Critic

Another tactic is naming your inner critic. That voice in your head that is super-mean and negative can feel a bit less daunting and scary with a name like "Bozo" or "Ebert the Self Critic." It also helps you to realize, once again, that you are not your thoughts. If you have a familiar thought pattern about one subject, you can give that a title as well. It is like coming up with a movie title, or a short story title, or maybe even a headline. See the examples below:

SELF TALK/TOPIC	NAME THE CRITIC/MOVIE/HEADLINE/ETC
Rumination over work project from last week	*Revenge of the Small Work Mistake Part III*
I feel like I don't fit in	*The My Friends are Cooler Than Me Radio Hour*
When I start assuming what other people think	*Breaking News: Girl Jumps to Conclusions Again*

CHAPTER 12 - Self-Compassion

Self-compassion is basically being kind to yourself, as you would have compassion or kindness for a stranger or a friend. Being kinder to yourself in general will help you have more positive self talk. In this chapter, we'll look at two strategies for self compassion.

Positive Affirmations

Like we talked about in Chapter 9, affirmations should be true things. For instance, don't tell yourself "I am a millionaire" if you are not. They should be things you know are true but have trouble telling yourself. Or use "May I" statements, as shown below. Then write out some affirmations of your own.

AFFIRMATIONS

I am worthy.	*May I feel beautiful today.*
I am a good person and people who know me would agree.	*May I be patient.*

Writing to a "Friend"

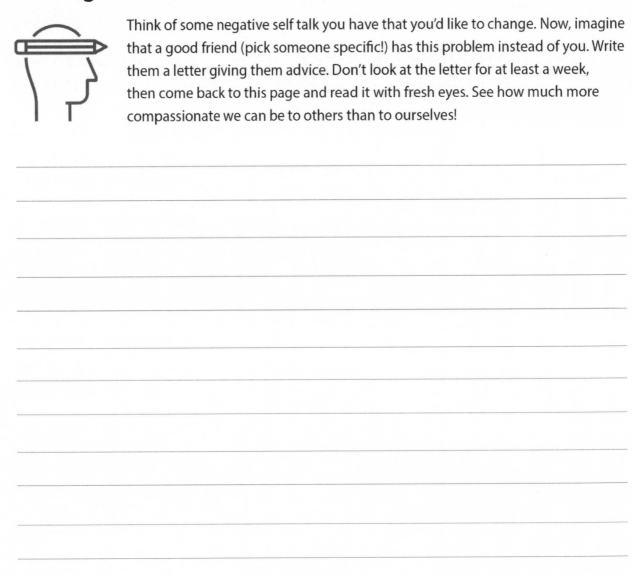

Think of some negative self talk you have that you'd like to change. Now, imagine that a good friend (pick someone specific!) has this problem instead of you. Write them a letter giving them advice. Don't look at the letter for at least a week, then come back to this page and read it with fresh eyes. See how much more compassionate we can be to others than to ourselves!

CHAPTER 13 - Constructive Negative Self Talk

"Positive thinking" has exploded in recent years as a world-wide phenomenon. But in this book, we aim for something more like "constructive thinking," "realistic thinking," or "optimistic thinking."

Your Inner Coach

Sometimes, our negative thoughts are just trying to help us become better, even if they have a cruel way of going about it. Maybe we **do** want to have healthier habits, but calling ourselves fat won't help! Instead of an inner critic, we need an inner coach or tough-love friend. They can support us changing the things we don't like about ourselves, but in a compassionate, supportive way that makes us feel good instead of bad. In this exercise, try reframing critical things about yourself into a pep talk from your inner coach.

INNER CRITIC	vs.	INNER COACH
I am not good at socializing		*I can improve my social skills with practice. Be brave!*
I get stressed too easily		*I am stressed right now, but it is temporary. Take a deep breath!*

CHAPTER 14 - Outside Influences

Though this book has obviously focused on what goes on in your head in terms of self talk, it wouldn't be complete without a mention of the other ways we can keep our brain healthy.

Meditation & Mindfulness

Meditation and/or mindfulness will really help you with being aware of your thoughts.

To meditate, download one of the many helpful meditation apps or try a free video on youtube. Or, just try to sit quietly for 5-10 minutes. Notice your thoughts, or try to maintain focus on your breath. Even one minute of meditation per day will help you de-stress.

To practice mindfulness, take a break several times a day to truly pay attention to the task at hand. Either practice breathing, or notice your senses. For example, if you are washing dishes, smell the soap, feel the warm water. If you are at work, notice the feel of the keyboard, the sounds of the office.

Diet & Exercise

The body and mind are intricately linked, so keeping your body healthy keeps your mind healthy.

You don't need to become a gym rat or health nut; even small changes make a big difference. Take the stairs instead of the elevator. Get a side salad with a burger instead of fries.

Where in your life can you make small changes today that will help your body and mind?

Social Circle

They say you are a the average of the five people you spend the most time with. So — what type of people are you surrounding yourself with?
Are they negative? Are they supportive? Do you think they have positive or negative self talk?

You should spend time with people you lift you up and make you feel better. Relationships are tricky, and beyond the scope of this book, but it is worth thinking about who may be holding you back from more positive self talk.

Social Media

Studies show that the more time people spend on social media, the unhappier they feel. Often, we are using social media to escape or distract ourselves from something.

Working on your self talk means you need time to *be* with your thoughts. If you have to wait in a grocery store line, practice not taking out your phone and scrolling, but practicing your self talk.

You'll be surprised how much time you can reclaim when you don't immediately pull out your phone at the first twinge of boredom.

The exercise on the next page for this chapter is a calendar. Choose from one of the categories we've discussed here and choose one tiny habit you can achieve for the next week. Make it as small as possible. If you make a huge goal — like going to the gym every day — it's hard to keep it up. But if you choose a small goal — like just putting on your running shoes once a day, even if it's just to get the mail — it will boost your confidence. Add on top of it one small goal the next week, and then another small goal the next week. The momentum of tiny goals can change your life! Use the calendar however you like. Just put a check mark if you did your goal, journal a bit, or do something else.

MY HABIT:

SUN	MON	TUE	WED	THU	FRI	SAT

MY HABIT:

SUN	MON	TUE	WED	THU	FRI	SAT

MY HABIT:

SUN	MON	TUE	WED	THU	FRI	SAT

MY HABIT:

SUN	MON	TUE	WED	THU	FRI	SAT

CHAPTER 15 - Conclusion

Thank you for reading this book and having the courage to go on a personal self talk journey. In this chapter, we have one last activity.

Looking Forward

Congratulations! The work in this book has been, I'm sure, very difficult at times. Thinking about our own thoughts is not easy, and what you have accomplished so far is something to be celebrated. In the following boxes, you'll reflect on what this journey has meant to you, and how you can continue making positive self talk a part of your life moving forward.

CELEBRATE! Draw, write, journal, whatever to celebrate finishing this book.
Be proud of yourself!

REFLECT. Now reflect on what you got the most out of from this book. What did you get the least out of ? Why?

WHAT DOES THE FUTURE LOOK LIKE? How can you take the practices you've learned into your every day life? What would you gain by doing so?

Please Let Me Know What You Thought

I would love to hear what you thought of this book.

Hearing that I've helped someone else is why I do what I do.

Please leave me a review on Amazon, as I read every one.

You can search your order history or the name of this book to find it again.

You can also reach me at aston@walnutpub.com.

Thank you so much, and good luck on the rest of your self talk journey.

-Aston

About the Author

Aston Sanderson is passionate about helping people lead better lives through short, conversational and fun books. He is the author of "Small Talk," a manual for better conversations, "Self Talk," a guide to practicing more self-love, and "Minimalist Living," a helpful way to declutter your life. He loves to hear from readers at aston@walnutpub.com for book feedback and ideas of what readers want to learn about next. His books are available in many languages worldwide.